ANTHOLOGY OF POETRY
BY
YOUNG AMERICANS®

2000 EDITION
VOLUME LXV

Published by Anthology of Poetry, Inc.

©*Anthology of Poetry by Young Americans*®
2000 Edition
Volume LXV

All Rights Reserved©

Printed in the United States of America

To submit poems
for consideration in the year 2001 edition of the
Anthology of Poetry by Young Americans®,
send to: poetry@asheboro.com or

        Anthology of Poetry, Inc.
        PO Box 698
        Asheboro, NC 27204-0698

Authors responsible
for originality of poems submitted.

The Anthology of Poetry, Inc.
307 East Salisbury • P.O. Box 698
Asheboro, NC   27204-0698

Paperback ISBN: 1-883931-25-8
Hardback ISBN: 1-883931-26-6

Anthology of Poetry by Young Americans®
is a registered trademark of
Anthology of Poetry, Inc.

As the new century dawns, the 2000 edition of the *Anthology of Poetry by Young Americans*® provides the fresh slate for the young minds that have shared thought and perspective with us over the past eleven years. In that time, we have witnessed the colorful expansion of the fabric of life, woven ever more brilliantly by poignant thought transferred to words, from the observant young people who have participated. It is through the senses of the young that we retain our youth, our optimism, and our curiosity. The eyes of our young have brought to our books vivid imagery; some as fine as a master impressionist, and others as frightening as the darkest storyteller. Their ears have played music for us page after page. Our children's sense of smell has sent us time traveling to the past, to some of our earliest memories. These young poets, through the sense of touch have reminded us' of the softest, safest feelings that our hands can remember. And from their young tongues, that have tasted for the first time the sweetness and bitterness of the small moments of life, we can savor the flavors of youth. The words and wisdom of these young poets have provided a collection of roadmaps for life. Just when we think we know the way, a small but accurate path is charted and handed to us by one of our children. It is to all of these poets that we owe the debt of thanks. We are expecting great things from them in the future.

The Editors

A TREE FOR ALL SEASONS

I stand proud and tall
Showing the radiance of my colors in the fall
People notice my glorious hues
A beautiful palette against a sky of blue

I stand bare and bold
A lonely skeleton in a land so cold
My limbs shiver and crack in the wind
I do not know how I can bend

I stand eager and surging
Healthy new growth is rapidly emerging
Fresh, tender sprouts tickle my bark
Each flowering bud makes its own special mark

I stand lush and strong
People seek my shady branches all day long
Resting thirsty roots on a carpet of green
A warm sunny day leaves me content and serene

Katie Barber
Age: 12

WHY ARE YOU SO SAD?

I was sitting in my room one day,
Thinking of those who wouldn't play.
I thought I had no friends out there;
I always thought they didn't care.

But God loved me -- I realized --
On the 27th I was baptized.
My life was suddenly turned around,
I knew that I was Heaven bound.

I soon had friends on every side,
Now, I didn't have to hide.
On my left and on my right,
Now they'll play from dawn 'til night.

Kristen Moore
Age: 12

FALL

Crisp bright leaves
Crunching on the ground
Red, orange, yellow and brown
Falling without a sound
Fall is the best season
Because you can make it into a mound!

Erin Toole
Age: 12

CHRISTMAS

The time for eggnog and hot chocolate is here,
So sit by the fire and have some great cheers.

For now is the time of the season,
To praise God for a great reason.

His son was born in a manger of hay,
There in the crib this blessed child lay.

Three wise men traveled from afar,
To bring him gifts in ornamented jars.

They brought him frankincense, myrrh, and gold,
A king was born was what they were told.

For it was that night that our Lord was born,
All the angels now play a great horn.

Oh! That starry night, what a glorious sight to see,
If I were there, I would have praised him on my knees.

Anna Criswell
Age: 13

THE FOREST FAIRY

I walked through the wood,
As silently as I could,
Acting very wary.

As I walked along,
I heard the song,
Of a tiny forest fairy.

I stopped to look,
For on the banks of the brook,
A light shone very bright.

I crept closer, ever nearer,
For I was a mesmerized hearer,
And the grasp of the song held me tight.

How long I listened I do not know,
Kneeling behind a bank of luminous white snow,
Not feeling the bite of cold.

Every word I understood,
Even though she spoke in the language of the Wood,
Describing all things of old.

She spoke of dragons with bejeweled wings,
And of the kind and just kings,
Who had long ago ruled the earth.

And I felt as if they had been my own good friends,
Though I know they had met their ends,
A long time before my birth.

She made me comprehend
What the humans have been doing,
And one day soon we would all be ruing,
If we did not build back what we had destroyed.

And how we no longer have a balance,
Because we had taken a dangerous chance,
When with nature we toyed.

So many beings have been killed,
And their blood spilled,
By those who have no right.

And how we are all obligated,
It can no longer be debated,
To solve our plight.

"Take the world in your hands,
Bring it back to its old state so grand,"
The fairy called out to me.

So today her message is passed on,
Now you too know of her song,
Someone must act now.
It is you? The task is urgent, can't you see?

Amanda Liscouski
Age: 13

COLOR

Yellow is
  a sunbeam reaching through a rain forest canopy.
Orange is
  leaves cracking as students run to school.
Maroon is
  the wine at church that lingers on the tongue
  ten minutes after drinking it.
Gray is
  the billowing fog slowly settling over the countryside.
Pink is
  a new piece of bubblegum, freshly unwrapped.

Diane Smith
Age: 13

Dog
cute, playful
eating, jumping, licking
soft against my face
Puppy

Brittany Jordan Seay
Age: 8

MY SISTER

My sister is a special person in my life
With hair of blonde and eyes of blue
She seems to be larger than life
Sometimes people can't tell who's who

She helps me when I need her
With my homework and other simple problems
I really love my sister
She is like a bag full of gems

She is my best friend
We are fourteen months apart
She won't leave me 'til the end
I care for her dearly in my heart

I love you like night and day
So please don't ever go away

Amanda Eileen Coyne
Age: 11

SPRING!

Spring is very fun,
The vis matrix naturae,
Power of nature!

Aaron W. Lewis
Age: 12

A SNOW DAY

The beautiful, fluffy snow,
Fell to the quiet earth one day.
The children could not go to school,
So they went outside to play.
Families went to chop down Christmas trees,
For they had plenty of time.
Many others had the same idea,
So everyone had to wait in a long line.
The peaceful, white snow kept falling down,
It got people into the friendly Christmas spirit.
Some children made tiny snow angels,
And others just dug in it.
A neighborhood sled race
was held on a huge, snow-covered hill,
People were having fun.
Even children raced adults,
And some fast children won.
After a cold but enjoyable day,
Everyone was ready to go.
The children's fathers carried home the trees,
To be decorated greatly they know.
The little children were sent to bed,
The older ones stayed up to help.
They decorated their trees
with tons of green and red tinsel,
That looked somewhat like kelp.
Carolers came to sing for enjoyment,
Their voices rose through the frosty air.
They sang only for fun and joy,
And because they care.
Now everyone is asleep in bed,

Even the oldest of men.
Each is dreaming happily,
And hoping for a snow day to come again.

Emily Tyndall
Age: 11

DREAMLAND

There is a place I know called Dreamland
Where a pleasant warm welcome will give you a hand
With blue sunny skies
And sweet butterflies,
With candy galore
No child would want more,
With treasures to behold
And stories untold,
People with China doll faces
And mystical, magical, never-seen places,
With forest filled with beautiful fairies
And forever-colorful blossom filled prairies,
With unicorns and fire-breathing dragons,
With delicate, golden, royal wagons,
Where kings and queens from everywhere
Come to celebrate, laugh, and share.
This wonderful place can come upon you.
Your imagination can lead you there too.

Mandana Nisanian
Age: 11

SNOW FELL

As the pearl-white snow
is falling calmly and softly
landing wherever the soft wind would take it,
kids and adults are ice-skating
throwing snowballs and sledding down hills
and squirrels and dogs are running in the snow.
Caroling heavenly songs.
Birds are flying in the air and landing
on a Christmas tree.
Snow is falling everywhere,
on trees, hills, roads, cars, and people
on Christmas morning.
It is tranquil. It's a beautiful white Christmas
all over again.
I wonder if next year's Christmas
will be the same wonderful white Christmas.

Torie Teague
Age: 11

Teacher
happy, nice
loving, caring, showing
helping me with work
Student!

Tonya Nichole Carthern
Age: 9

ORANGE

Orange refreshes like juices from a big ripe orange.
Orange crackles like embers of a dying campfire.
Orange splatters like a paintball on a blank white wall.
Orange tickles with a pungent citrus fragrance.
Orange warms me like the bright sun
After a cold winter rain.

Eric Schultz
Age: 13

A LONG-LOST FRIEND

For him, I wait, and wait, and wait
I know he'll come, I know!
Even though he is two days late,
I wait for him still so.

Today I received a short letter;
It was from the leader, Sergeant Don Juan.
It didn't make me feel much better;
I was told my friend was forever gone.

Now I sit and wonder why,
Why did it happen to me?
Now I sit and now I cry,
Now all alone I will be.

Kayla Bly
Age: 12

WHAT I DON'T WANT TO BE

I can't be what I don't want to be.
If I be what I don't want to be.
It's terrifying to me.

Milad Soufastai
Age: 9

RED

The color of love,
    That makes you feel good inside.
Roses' fragrance floating about the earth,
    Suddenly the thorns tear through the fingers.
Cherries, pliant and clasped in the hands,
    Of a baby eating a pie.
Water from a watermelon swishing in the mouth,
    A few seeds here and there.
Cardinals fly by searching for food,
    The fledglings still in the nest.
The sonant of Christmas music suspended in the air,
    Kids opening presents under the tree.
There are the things I think about,
    When I think of the beautiful color red.
There are the things I think about,
    When I think of the beautiful color red.

Mark Harkins
Age: 13

FATE

According to the Bible we are all being judged;
Above us, God is evaluating our performance
  as Christians.
Beneath us, Satan is judging the failure of believers;
They are waiting for the day when judgment is at hand.

From place to place around the world,
Beyond our own shadows,
For obscure reasons we continue to endure the pain
  of judging one another.
We assess our fellow man using explanations
such as nationality or race.

Behind masks that civilization has created,
Within our innermost souls we are paranoid
Of the magnates of high society
Who judge everyone throughout eternity.

In spite of the great devastation and grief
judgment has caused,
Upon only our arrival to Heaven,
Among the beautiful angels' wings,
Will we realize what anguish judgment has caused.

Brianne Marie Wesolowski
Age: 12

TO RECALL

One's mind is divided, into not one but two parts,
Each holding a specific purpose, one to do
  and one to know what has been done.
One's mind holds a savior and a ceaseless hinder;
It holds the greatest things we have ever done
  and the mistakes that can shame one forever.
But one's memory can never be lied to;
Some have been driven down the dark path
  of the mad for this very reason,
For one can be abusive to his recollections;
A mind can never be taken for granted
  and never should be told anything
  that one would not want to experience again,
Though the good memories of one's past
  may be harder to unlock;
In the eternal labyrinth of a memory, an epic search
  can be conducted to find the good in one's past,
But most hold the hell of an oppressive guilt
  close at hand;
As it has been observed that most
  of the one's final thoughts are of guilt,
  why bother to find the lost pride of one's success?
Memory can be the greatest blessing ever to be held
  to one's soul,
Or it can be a horrifying curse
  to the depths of one's mind.

The mere use of such a gift is at the discretion
    of those who practice it;
The constant battle goes on as a memory fights time
    and common hatred,
As the power of one's memory is measured by his will
    to believe in true acceptance
    from the reality he exists in.

Matt Drake
Age: 14

THE SENSE OF SUMMER

Yellow is the sun's warm rays touching your cheeks
    at the beach,
Blue is the salt water in your mouth
    after an unexpected wave crashes on your face,
Beige is the sand castle that seems perfect in your mind
    but never turns out just right,
White is the stench of suntan lotion
    holding you back from diving into the hotel's pool,
Brown is the screeching of the putrid pelicans
    keeping you awake at night.

Allison Shirley
Age: 14

LIFE IN GOD

Life, it starts by His grace,
It ends with the sweep of His omnipotent hand.
It's gone before we know it,
But what exactly is it?

As the morning dew descends upon the grass,
The sun reveals itself from the shadows
of the eastern mountains.
Color after color shoots through the sky,
Painting a picture that could not possibly be captured
onto any other canvas than God's.

The world pauses for a brief moment
As the wonderful dreams come to a halt.
All nightmares are abruptly ended,
And God's day begins.

The familiar chirping of birds echoes
throughout the valley,
But today a new cry is heard.
It is not one of a bird, or rooster.
This morning, it is the cry of God's miracle.

God watched from the sacred heavens
As His creation grew and developed in Him.
The baby was protected from demonic acts
and unpredictable accidents,
For this is the way God planned it to be.

The child grew to be an adult,
Now, with his name in THE BOOK OF LIFE,
He devoted his entire life to God.

He stored his treasures not on earth,
but above the clouds, while God watched them develop.

Finally the morning came,
As in the morning, all dreams and nightmares ended,
But this time they ended along with the man's life.
The heavens split with a thunderous crack,
And heavenly trumpets could be heard
far off in the distance.
The man's soul was lifted to be with God,
Where he shall not perish, but have everlasting life.
A life far greater than the most luxurious life on earth.
Do not fear death, for if you ask, God will secure a place
for you in Heaven.

Daniel Baily
Age: 13

HALLOWEEN

Close the windows, lock the doors!
Here come the ghosts, goblins, witches and wargs!
Ha, Ha! and Boo! are the sounds that I hear,
Louder and louder as evil grows near.
I stare out the window in pure fright
I looked for anything odd in the night.

Courtney Quiros
Age: 12

The autumn breeze
Lifts a wisp of hair
As goose bumps form on my arms

Scores of leaves
Awake, rustle as I walk

Brilliant hues of gold
Streak the sky
The sun says her last good-bye

A gust of frigid air
Reminds me
That autumn is alive

I dodge plummeting leaves
My breath condenses
And is lost in the wind

The darkness now engulfs me
I imagine things unseen

Something is behind me
Petrified huffs of breath escape me
I start to run, but stagger

I fall to my knees
The stench of decayed leaves
Submerges my hysteria

I bawl uncontrollably
Wishing for death
Not waiting for what's to come

Sucking for life
The sudden silence is deafening
And I hear a faint cry of triumph

For it was nothing behind me
Only the whisper of wind

Colette Hartman
Age: 14

GREEN

Fresh as the morning;
As cool as the fall breeze in those early hours.
Glistening like dew on freshly-cut grass,
Shimmering, sparkling.
Like the sweet scent of herbs from the garden;
Sharpening the senses like an army commander
keeps his soldiers in line.
Calming like rain --
Slow and gradual, yet persistent.
Refreshing as an ice-cold, lemon-lime Powerade
after a tiring soccer game.
Desolate, like a pine in a large, obscure forest.
Standing out as easily as a maple in a field of shrubs,
High above the rest, like the Yankees;
The best of them all!

Danny O'Shaughnessy
Age: 13

A BLINDED WALK

Through the mist I walk with blurred vision,
An irridescent white wall is lain before me
I am guided by my clumsy hands;
Like a bat
My fingers are my radar;

I hear the flowers
Dancing in the breeze;
I hear the birds
Watching from the trees;

I smell the dew;
I smell the mist;
Their fresh scent fuses through the forest;

I feel the damp grass under my feet;
I feel the thick morning air filling my lungs;
I feel, I see, I hear the morning
As I walk blinded by the morning mist.

Amanda Petersson
Age: 13

BLISS

As I lie on the cool ground, leaves rustle all around me.
Flying through the air they seem to whisper my name
so quietly.
Only people that listen hard can hear it.
As I look towards the heavens a gentle breeze
rids me of all my problems.
The breeze grows stronger and tosses my hair
whichever way it pleases.
The wind has no owner, no master,
and no one to control it.
The high-pitched chirping of birds fills the cool air.
I feel as if I am in another world or dimension.
It is a perfect place with no problems of reality.
So calm and peaceful.
Like in a fairy tale your mother read to you as a baby,
it is a perfect place.
My perfect place, a refuge, and a shelter,
somewhere I can escape to.
This perfect place is, my perfect place is bliss.

Kevin Hood
Age: 11

NIGHTTIME

I don't like going to bed.
I think it's bad for my head.
On Christmas I like to stay up
And see Santa's sled.
Same with my friend Ned.
I used to play dead with my dog Ted.
I don't like going to bed.

Adam Stimpert
Age: 8

MY FAVORITE PLACE

Yellowstone National Park:
Hiking, exploring and adventuring
It reminds me of how we live in a complex world
It shows me that nature is the true example for all
It calms my mind and sets serenity in my soul
It makes any other park look like a polluted wasteland
It is wonderful, yet you'll never be able to see it all
It is majestic and strong
It is huge and it makes your backyard seem tiny
It will stay in your mind forever
Yellowstone National Park:
Sightseeing, discovering and learning.

Robert Banick
Age: 11

ALONE IN THE DARK

Alone in the dark
She is determined not to fail
Alone in the dark
She finally learned Braille
Alone in the dark
Her love for Annie grew
Alone in the dark
A whole other world she never knew
Alone in the dark
One person kept her up
Alone in the dark
Annie never gave up
Alone in the dark
The word water became light
Alone in the dark
She had her own kind of sight
Alone in the dark she made her way
Alone in the dark
She took each step day-by-day.

Christine Lee Dozier
Age: 14

WEIRD BABOON

A baboon is weird
So is a banana
Along with the monkey in the zoo
With the ants crawling about
Eating the sugars one by one
The weird things among the world
The baboon is the weirdest of them all

Hayes Crowley
Age: 10

MY MOM

When I think of my mom
I think of the sound of her voice
waking me up in the morning
I think of the touch of her soft skin
when she gives a hug to dry my tears
I think of the light scent of her perfume
that she wears to church
I think of the sight of her
when the dog wakes her up in the morning
I think of the taste of the pasta at dinnertime
My mom is special to me
I love her
She is my best friend
My mom.

Christina Hoff
Age: 12

AUTUMN

Days at the beach and hot humid days
are locked away with summer.
A chill arouses in the midst of transition.
And lemonade stands, as well as drippy ice cream cones
become distant, yet cherished memories.
Autumn has arrived.
Leaves transform into pure hues of golden, crimson,
and sun-orange.
They fall from the heavens above like a mass
of irridescent sprinkles, descending into cake-like yards,
Where children parade in snug jackets with rakes at hand
Autumn has arrived.
A cool brisk breeze drifts through the frosty air.
As the aroma of apple pie and pumpkin bread
wafts beside.
A light fire and a warm mug of hot apple cider
accessorizes homes
along jack-o'-lantern-lit roads.
Autumn has arrived.

Mary Lyons
Age: 13

LIFE

Life
Has meaning,
In a way.
But does it?

What happens
When you die?
Do you go to Heaven,
Hell,
Or do you just stop living?

What would happen
If you lived forever?
Would life
Have texture,
Solid and real,
Or would it
Be a bore?

What can happen
When you're alive?
Can you help
Someone in need,
Or can you just sit
And complain?

What will happen
In your life?
Will you go to college
And marry,
Or will you work
At McDonald's always?

What you know,
Can be what you are,
But you have
To want it
And work at it.

Using your heart,
Mind,
And soul,
Together,
Can make
Life
A better place
For you.

Nicky Capell
Age: 13

MOM

She loves me
  And takes care of me
Red hair and brown eyes
  Brown skin
She wears clogs
  And hearts of gold on her ears.

Anissa Neal
Age: 6

MY OWN UNIVERSE

Clouds glide smooth in one swirling mass.
This ocean in the sky makes a slow gliding pass.
Beauty in the grays, beauty in the blues,
Traces of white and starlit hues.
A gap in the darkness, a crack in the dome.
A twinkle of Orion as he peers towards my home.
This strong and mighty giant fills the night sky.
I see his face in far-off space and quietly wonder why,
Why the stars fill shapes of men and beast,
Portraits painted from west to east,
A beautiful picture beyond the pictures
Of clouds and sky.
Again I ask why,
For us this all was created,
And it is this we truly have wasted.
Thrown to the wind, the beauty within,
Instead of seeking, we squandered for sin.
Destruction and creation: too much of one;
Of the other, too little or none.
Why create for myself when I can destroy for more.
With key of hate we open most selfish of doors.
Pompous, we stray,
And misguided we say,
Anything for me.
Everything for free.

THEXPOET

Andrew Senter

There once was a woman named Kym.
She took her dog to the gym.
Lifting weights he built his body,
He bacame a tough little Scotty.
Now strong and trim, no one messes with him.

Morgan Libbey
Age: 10

GOD

I heard someone knocking at my heart's door,
And I looked to see that it was God.
I knew right away that I couldn't let Him in
Because my heart was so dirty from the stains of sin.
Jealousy hung on the walls;
Lying and cheating littered the halls;
Envy hung on a shelf
Along with bad grades that I put there, myself.
Hatred was scattered all around;
Murder and robbery could even be found.
God kept knocking but what could I do?
It was too dirty for God to come in;
Wait another day and come back again.
Let me clean it up the best that I can.
God kept knocking at my heart's door.
I opened the door and He was faithful and true.
He cleaned it right up; now everything is new.

Cheryce Dunklin
Age: 13

THE STORM

The rain pitter-patters
Down silver gutters.
The storm will never end!
But then I see,
Miraculously,
The sun brightly shining down on me!

As I splash in the puddles
I laugh and make merry.
For everyone knows
'Tis the season of cherries.

Mariana Marcuse
Age: 10

BOOKS

A book is something read by heart.
It's divided in chapters, part by part.
Read it wisely... read it well.
Listen as it captures you in a deep, dark spell.
A book is read thoroughly in and out.
It is read with the heart without a doubt.
So read it wisely... read it well.
It is something with power... a story to tell.

Jessica Hormann
Age: 9

FOOTBALL

Football is a very good sport
Some football players go to court
They went because they did bad things
Some hit others with rings

Scott Curtiss
Age: 10

BROUGHT TO A STANDSTILL

A glass of Remy Martin
On the coffee table.
Three-year-old coffee,
Unopened, napping in the cupboard.
Guitar resting against the wicker chair
Near the fireplace, tuned
Exactly one year ago.
A day-old sandwich is lying
Out on the window sill
With only one bite taken out of it.
Nothing makes a noise save the
Deafening ticking of the second hand
On the somber grandfather clock.
A push of the pause button
Doesn't make a difference;
Even peopled surroundings go unnoticed.

Meiling Arounnarath
Age: 16

31

BUBBLEGUM GOO

Bubblegum goo is stuck on my shoe
Stuck on my shoe is bubblegum goo
It is sticky, icky, gooey, and ooey
It is very very chewy
But however much I chew and chew
It is still bubblegum, bubblegum goo

Rebecca Haney
Age: 11

FOOTBALL GAMES

I run
I cheer
I scream
I yell
I taste greasy
onion rings
I play football,
tag,
and
hide-and-go-seek.
I absolutely
LOVE
football games.

Mary Elizabeth Trapani
Age: 9

THE CASTLE

It's an old haunted castle.
The graveyard... full.
It was a full moon...
The dungeon empty.
The cannons still and silent.
Flags flapping in the wind.
Not a live fish in the pond.
See the Milky Way...
Millions of miles away.
The doors locked tightly
The croc's sleeping in the moat.
Not a LIFE in sight WAIT!
The croc's waiting for someone
To be foolish enough...
To go into the moat.
To be eaten up.
So beware...
Don't jump in any moats
Around an old castle...
During a full moon.

Adolphus Kyle Estes
Age: 11

ICE-SKATING

Winning seems golden
Like happiness
I see my coach
I smell the flowers
I touch my skates
I taste victory

Ken Shigley Jr.
Age: 10

PEAS!

Peas are nasty.
Peas are green.
Peas are stinky.
Peas are mean.

Peas are wrinkled.
Peas are round.
Peas are soft.
Peas are round.

Peas are tasteless,
And you can't eat peas in a cup
Peas are slimy,
And if you ever see a pea say yuk!!

Nyland A. Jenkins
Age: 11

HORSES

There is nothing more graceful than a horse.
Their manes and their tails flying in the wind.
The sun or the moon shining on their glossy coats.
There is nothing more graceful than a horse.

Elizabeth Valocchi
Age: 9

NATURE

The sky looks like a sea of blue,
With dots of soft, fluffy cotton balls.

Down below,
The scent of tall, skinny
Evergreens fills the air
And tingles your nose.

On the branches,
Dark charcoal crows
Screech out cries of hunger.

The yellow honey
Drips out of a beehive
And tastes thick and sweet on your tongue.

Sara Thompson
Age: 13

WHAT I WANT

I want to be in the world.
Be part of the good and apart from the bad.
I want to get dirty, be freezing
and comforted by my mother's warmth.
I want to play with my dolls
and have tea parties when I am little.
I want to be left a kid, but then I
want to grow up and be all I can
be and whatever I want to be.
I want to be allowed to learn all
the knowledge from all the books
in the world.
I don't want to be made fun of or teased.
I want to be recognized for what
I do right and the things I do wrong forgotten.
I want to be a mother of children.
I want to defend them, be part of their life
and not left out.
I want to be a grandmother and be proud
of my family and them be proud of me.
I want to be old but young in the heart.
I want to have a big house in the country,
where I can wade my feet in the stream
and catch and free butterflies, frogs, and fireflies.
I want to be a kid again when I'm old.
Most of all I want to
LIVE MY OWN LIFE!

Rebecca Sellers
Age: 11

When I think of Katie,
I see a person of influence and love.
She influences me in everyway.
She is my idol,
My sister;
She is my friend;
She is a person of wisdom, wonder and thought,
She wonders along in the world of wonder,
Thinks along in the world of thought,
Loves along in the world of love.
She is my idol,
She is my sister,
She is my friend.
The way she thinks,
The way she laughs,
The way she loves.
The way she is
Is always hers,
Always Katie's
Always.

Megan E. Brigham
Age: 11

ANGELS

They fly around your bed at night,
They go back up in a faint light,
To Heaven above where they belong,
Like flying doves, singing a song.

They help a bird,
And a baby fawn,
They pray to God,
At the crack of dawn.

Then they went to find all their children,
That they were guardian angels to,
A couple of them were Frank and Sally,
Two of them were Tom and Sue.

Then a shout came from Gabriel,
As he put his hands on a table,
When he yelled, "Silence"
And his sound went over the golden fence.

Hurry! We must bring gifts,
To our newborn king!
Hurry! Don't you know?
It's Christmas morning.

Elizabeth Hanna

FATHER

When I think of my father
I picture someone just glad to be who they are
He is always glad to get up in the morning
and take his children to school
He is a person more than happy to work hard
He's someone who can comfort and care for me
Someone who can cheer me up when I'm blue
From him I've learned to accept myself
No I may not be the prettiest, brightest, or nicest,
But just as long as when I get up in the morning
I know that the day before I did my best
To be all that I am capable of and achieving
I can say that I'm worth it
Just because I am not any big-time person
doesn't mean I'm not important
God loves you
And then there are all the fathers in the world
that love you
So tonight try extra hard to see the person your dad is
After all he does love you

Ashton M. Bligh
Age: 12

MY DAD

When I think of my dad,
I picture a Sunday morning,
The smells of bacon and his famous hash browns,
A beautiful morning,
The smells of a new day beginning,
My father is home,
This day will be great,
We'll spend time together,
We'll play basketball and maybe some catch,
A wonderful day spent with my father.

Rachel Kravitz
Age: 13

DOGS

Dogs are cute.
Dogs are warm.
Sometimes dogs can bite.
Dogs can learn tricks.
Dogs need food to live.
Dogs need water to live.
Dogs need lots of love.
I love my dog.

Anna Elise Wren
Age: 8

DAD:

When I think of my dad
I think of love, encouragement and running
My dad runs every day
He runs for events where you run
My dad encourages me all the time
He tells me to study a lot
Because he wants me to go to Harvard
He also tells me to go the extra mile for everything
My dad loves me so much
Every day when he gets home from work he hugs me
And asks how my day was

Dan Galvez
Age: 13

HALLOWEEN

You see bats at Halloween.
The fun thing is you get candy.

Pumpkins are carved.
That means it is Halloween.

Sometimes if you look carefully
You see an owl.

Jesse Hewes Ihns
Age: 5

LIZ

When I think of my sister
I hear the smell the scent of her sweet perfume,
and see her luscious hair
The way she sings and laughs so soft
reminds me of her beauty inside that seems so fair
She looks after me and takes me by the hand
through the hard and despairing times
She is kind to me and whispers in a way
just as a swaying chime

Her love for me and my love for her
makes us so complete
If we live again, in another way,
I know that we shall meet

We may quarrel and we may bicker
and fight in a hurtful way
But the love we have for each other
will conquer over this for every single day

Stephanie Sizemore
Age: 12

42

THE CHILD

She is a little spoiled mess
She fiddles with her lovely dress
But when she lies upon her bed
She feels that she has not been fed.

Her big royal room will shimmer
Her little fortune will dimmer
And when she finds she has no love
She will always be a dove.

When she was a beautiful mother,
She had one man or no other
With a daughter bright as the sun
She and her family had lots of fun.

Now she's a nice grandma
With lots of sweets
She will always have treats
She has a nice gigantic house,
With only 9,000,000,990 rooms.

She's had a lovely life
As a child, grandma, and wife
And as she lay upon her deathbed
Rest is all that's in her head.

Elizabeth M. Stamps
Age: 11

THORNY DEVIL

Sense
Smell
taste, draw near
small ant
Big ant
hot desert.
Thirsty
not am I
pant
rest. Big hole
sleep
yes I am

Aaron Hobbs
Age: 10

VALENTINE

Roses are red
Violets are blue
Make a happy valentine
That says I love you.
Give this happy valentine
To your mom or dad
Give this happy valentine
To anyone.
I am sure they will be glad.

Catherine Kelsey Sharp
Age: 9

Country
quiet, beautiful
farming, ranching, cultivating
shopping, marketing, factory working
noise, busy
City

Laura Michelle Bennett
Age: 10

CLOUDS

Clouds are white,
Clouds are gray,
Clouds are pink.

When clouds are white
There is no fright.

When clouds are gray
A storm's a-coming.

When clouds are pink
The sun could be setting.

James Vance Schearback II

FLAMES

flames are hot
flames are red
flames will burn
flames will spread
flames will scold
flames will burn down something really old
flames are yellow
flames say HELLO when you sit on them
the only cure for these fellows is icy-cold water

Dusty Beasley

MY COUSIN'S HORSES

My cousin has four horses.
Next to her house in Connecticut.

She now rides and jumps.
I rode on some ponies at fairs.
I wish I could be in some horse races.

I dream about being at my cousin's house
Doing jumps with horses.

Robbie Reynell
Age: 5

NATURE

Nature is lovely --
Mountains rise above the seas
The sun shines brightly

Benjamin James Morris
Age: 9

DONNELLAN, OH DONNELLAN

Donnellan, oh Donnellan you sure are cool.
I wish I could be as cool as you.
You are everything a school should need.
Man, Donnellan, you are really neat.
School rules with you.
Donnellan you are so very awesome.
I'm glad my parents sent me to this school.
It's the best place you'll ever be,
Especially with our principal.
It has a neat library and a cafeteria,
Plus it's got a field and playground,
And it's got a science lab.
Donnellan is the best place to be.
So come with me and come to Donnellan.

Meghan Livermore
Age: 8

MY ROOM

My room is special to me.
My bed is hot.
My room feels good!

Samuel Paul Walchko
Age: 6

THE SEA

Oh, the sea is big as can be
with lots of creatures to meet you and me.
Some are big, some are small,
you just can't see them all.

There are some that are dangerous
and some that are not.
There are some that are in danger
and others that are not.

Oh, the sea is as calm as can be,
and then maybe not.
The sea needs care
and the sea needs help.
The sea is polluted
and yet there is no one to help,
but maybe there is.

Amber Marie Cowart
Age: 11

WHAT MAKES ME DIFFERENT

I look like my dad,
when he is glad.
He is tall and I am short.
He is friendly and I am shy
but I am the apple of his eye.

Eric Thigpen
Age: 9

MOVING

Pack up!
Kelly is moving
To Florida
The class is staying here.
Her house is not coming
To Florida.
Mommy and Daddy and Bobby and Erin
Are coming
To Florida.
There is a flat ground
And not many cars.
I miss everybody that I like
At my school in Florida
The boys scream on the playground.

Kelly Berger
Age: 4

Horses are beautiful
Horses are very very fast and fun
They sparkle in the sunlight
And their glorious stride brightens
Horses I very much love and adore!

Allison M. Holton
Age: 11

Up on the moon.
Down on a room.
Pop! Pop! Up in the air.
Boo! Boo! Scare you!

Mallory Riner
Age: 6

HALLOWEEN

Tonight is the night when dead leaves fly
like witches on switches across the sky.
Tonight all the ghosts and goblins come around.
Then all the ghosts holler BOO
because tonight is Halloween.
At midnight all the skeletons come around
and run all night throughout the town.
Because tonight is Halloween.

Melissa Gresham

I LOVE CATS

I love cats
They have wet little noses
They are very sweet
Furry little babies
Cool little colors
Little little feet
Sharp little nails
Purring all the time
Always there to cuddle
I love cats

Danielle Brass
Age: 10

THANKSGIVING

Thanksgiving is a time of celebration,
My grandmothers come for a vacation.
My mom, dad, brother, and I,
Always go around wanting to spy.
We have a big turkey to enjoy while we eat,
My little dog sits there acting so sweet.
He wants my huge pancake,
But my mom won't let him take.
Thanksgiving is a fun day,
But I want my grandmothers to stay.

Kristin Danielle Zipperer
Age: 11

THANKSGIVING

Thanksgiving what a joyous time
  Now I have to type a poem that rhymes.
Every year we go to Grandmother's,
  My sister and my brothers.
We eat turkey, ham, and candied yams
  Maybe this year we'll try some lamb.
What a great holiday to eat and get full.
  Then we feel like fat bulls.

Amber Baldwin
Age: 9

BECAUSE OF YOU AND ME...

The woolly mammoth is extinct it's easy to see
The woolly mammoth is extinct because of you and me.
We didn't protect our environment
so this is what we get.
A world full of house pets and animals
we don't know of yet.
What has happened to our animals
I'm very sad to say
all the animals have died or had to go away.
I like animals and I hope you do too.
But to save our animals it is up to me and you.

Charlee Lynn Russell
Age: 10

SIGNS OF THANKSGIVING

When November comes around,
   The leaves start to fall down.
The falling leaves crunch,
   And soon it's time for lunch.
We thank the Lord for all our blessings,
   Then we eat the turkey and dressing.
We see our family for the day,
   And all the children get to play.

Slaton Christopher Owens
Age: 9

THE TRADITION OF THANKSGIVING

The tradition of Thanksgiving
is family and friends gathered together
eating turkey, dressing and cranberry sauce.
It tastes so good you seem to get lost.
Macaroni and cheese and string beans too,
all are so tasty I don't know what to do.
Your belly is so full you lie on the couch,
all night long all you do is slouch,
that's what Thanksgiving is all about.

Chianti Cone
Age: 10

CATS

Cats have soft fur.
  They like to purr.
They like to play with a yarn ball.
  They need their fur because it gets cold in the fall.
Some are skinny some are fat.
  My cat likes to lie on the mat.
Cats can be lazy.
  My cat's name is Daisy.

Joanna Dorton
Age: 11

THE GAME

I'm at the bat,
  Boy that pitcher sure is fat,
I'm going to hit it in the field,
So shortstop you better yield,
  I'm going to hit it so far,
It may melt and turn into tar,
  What did the umpire say?
Oh, three strikes what a day!

Ashley E. Joyner
Age: 11

BIRTH OF A COLT

When a colt is born,
It comes out in a wet sack
That has to be cut.

Zachary Taylor Sadler
Age: 10

Thanksgiving is a day for giving, caring and sharing
Thanksgiving is a day for forgiving and reliving

Thanksgiving is a day for being thankful
For all the food we eat
Thanksgiving is a day for giving special treats

And if I was the President and had my way
Thanksgiving would be a standard of living every day.

Andre Waters
Age: 10

THE CREEPS

At night there's ponder
there is no wonder
but they all creep
while you sleep.

Rusty Beasley

WHAT PARENTS ARE FOR

Parents are wonderful people.
Your parents take care of you.
When you get hurt, they're there.
When you have a bad dream, parents are there.
Every time you don't understand,
Parents are there to help you.
So be thankful that you have parents,
Because some people don't.

"I've got WONDERFUL PARENTS."

Cory Samples
Age: 10

TRACTOR

Tractor, tractor where are you?
Tractor, tractor I see you.
Tractor, tractor you are so bright
And out of sight.
Tractor, tractor you look so mighty.
Tractor, tractor big and green.
Tractor, tractor you look so mean.
Tractor, tractor you are so
Powerful.

Nicholas C. Benton
Age: 11

My brother is nice.
My brother is sweet.
My brother makes me smile,
Like a very nice treat.
He is cute and he is neat,
My brother I really want to keep.

Meredith Moore
Age: 10

LOVE

L is for the way I'm never Lonely
O is for the Oath I took to love everyone
V is for Victory we have won
E is for the Everlasting love God gave me.

Brittany Laine Bellflower
Age: 10

YOUR PERSONALITY

In the mall...
In the streets...
Even in a mansion...

You're still the same person inside.

Victoria Reynolds

Friend
loyal, trustworthy
loving, giving, understanding
A friend makes me feel loved.
Pal

Emily Vinson
Age: 10

Studying
work, recess
running, eating, working
Studying makes me feel good.
Analyze

Adam Stribling
Age: 9

BASEBALL

Summer, winter, spring, or fall,
I can't wait to play baseball.
Like all the seasons take their place,
Then I will be playing at first base.

Patrick Blaine Allen

Why didn't you tell me?
I told you drugs were bad
if you would have followed my lead,
then you wouldn't be dead.

I told you that I loved you
and everything was going to be all right,
but you never seemed to listen
so you weren't here to live through that night.

I guess I pushed you too hard
for you to follow my lead,
but deep down inside
I guess I didn't know your need.

If you were here right now,
I would have made sure you knew you were loved.
Everybody has got their own problems
but I thought you were going above.

I'm sorry I let you down,
I just wanted to know
how I could have helped you
so that you wouldn't have had to go.

I'm sorry it ended up like this
but I got to let you go.
I thought it was my fault
but now I will never know.

Leigh Brannon
Age: 12

J oltin' Joe nickname
O nly man to hit safely in fifty-six games straight
E lected to Hall of Fame

D ivorced Marilyn Monroe on October 27, 1954
I n 1931 quit Galieo High School in tenth grade
M VP three times in his career
A warded US Medal of Freedom given by President Ford
G iusseppe and Rosalie Paolo DiMaggio were his parents
G iven the name Greatest Living Player
I n his career played in ten World Series
O n November 25, he and six of his seven kids were born

Paige Wade

R oger Clemens was born August 4, 1962
   in Dayton, Ohio.
O ften likes to go to sunny resorts.
G enerous with his family.
E xcellent father and husband.
R ocketman is his nickname.

C atches good fly balls.
L oves his family.
E xcellent baseball player.
M ost successful in his career.
N olan Ryan is his all-time favorite player.
S wimming is one of his favorite things to do off-season.

Erika M. Balderas
Age: 12

Crisp cool air's blowing,
Witches, brooms, bats, and pumpkins,
Ghost stories scare me!

Haley Nicole Atterholt
Age: 10

Dogs
furry, funny
fetching, scratching, chewing
Dogs make me feel excited,
because they are usually very playful and fun.
Puppies

Sara Nissly
Age: 10

OCEAN

Ocean
fish, seashells
fishing, swimming, taking
The ocean makes me feel cold.
Sea

Ansley Addlesburger

F all is over
A ll is clear
L ine up the coats
L ine up the snow

I s it gone
S hould we see

O n the boots
V ote for me
E nter the cold
R un up and down

Because fall
is over!

Rachael D. Larington
Age: 11

BUTTERFLIES

Butterflies
fluttery, colorful
flying, floating, dancing
blowing up and down
through the trees and up
into the great blue sky
Insects

Amanda Nissly
Age: 10

FALL

When it is fall the trees are blowing,
and the cool breeze is carrying the leaves
across my yard.

The weather can change to whatever it wants to,
but it is usually cold.

At night I cuddle up under the covers
with my teddy bear.
I love my teddy, and I love fall!

Victoria James
Age: 7

SIGNS OF THANKSGIVING

Thanksgiving is near;
It is quite clear.
Leaves are on the ground;
Fun to rake them up, then drown.
Turkeys roast on the open fire;
The object of our desire.
Food, food, food galore;
Fruits, pies, cakes, and more!

Rachel Bowers
Age: 9

FLOWERS

I like flowers.
I hope you do too!
Flowers are cool and so are you.

Katie Barber
Age: 7

LOVE

Flowers are pretty,
So are you.
I love Ben S.
I hope you do too.
He is cute,
So are you.

Lauren Clark
Age: 7

YELLOW

Yellow is a bumblebee flying by me.
Yellow is a sunflower blowing in the wind.
Yellow is a French fry getting eaten.

Alexander G. Harbeson

BIRDS

Birds, birds, high in the sky,
Singing away. Oh my, oh my!
Their songs I love to hear in the day
In May.

Birds are beautiful creatures,
Red, blue, and yellow,
And all kinds of designs.

Birds love to perch on trees,
And sing all day, pretty please.
They perch on my window and sing away
All day.

I like to see birds play in water.
Splash, splash, splash and all day, all day.
Birds play in the trees.
Tweet, tweet, tweet, away.

Birds sing beautiful songs.
They sing so many,
I don't know with which to sing along.

Kayla Wood
Age: 8

NAME ABOVE ALL NAMES

I will look to You always Adonai;
I am consumed by the flame of Your light.
My life is to serve You oh Lord most high.
Oh bright Morning Star who has pierced the night.
Prince of Peace, my Comforter in sorrow.
Jehovah, the Spring of Living Water.
One who brings new joy with each tomorrow.
The Creator, the Maker, the Potter.
My Protector, my Rock, my hiding place.
Alpha, Omega, the Author of Life.
Father of Mercy and amazing grace.
One who carries me through all pain and strife.
A shade from the heat, my strength and my friend.
Eternal God, the Beginning and End.

Lindsey M. Dunagan
Age: 16

DOGGY, DOGGY

Doggy, doggy do you like your bone?
Doggy, doggy are you at home?
Doggy, doggy where are you?
Doggy, doggy I want to see you.
Doggy, doggy there you are.
I love you!

Laura Grant
Age: 7

CATS

Some cats are black.
Some cats are blue.
Some cats are red,
and they really stink too!
They have so many mice,
and they are so nice.
They have balls and yarn,
but the best of all live in barns,
chasing bats all around the yard.
Cats are wild.
Some cats are mild.
Some cats are made of clay,
and they stay in your house and never play.
There are so many different cats,
and this is the end of that.

Phuong Nguyen
Age: 8

BLUE

Blue is as colorful as the shiny sky.
Blue is as wonderful as a shirt.
Blue is a place where there is water
And it's hard to get hurt.
Blue is as blue as a blueberry, but not a cherry.
Blue is cool because it's not true that blue is a cool fool.

Edward Lee Baker
Age: 7

WAITING

He sat quietly by the bog
Waiting, waiting, peering through the fog.
What he was waiting for, I'm not quite sure.
Wait -- someone said he was waiting for her.

She was a beautiful girl of sixteen
Her hair a deep brown, her eyes flashing green.
She was popular, pretty and smart.
Her passions were in drawings and art.

He had blue eyes, hair black as a crow
He felt like an outcast, had nowhere to go.
They met one day, fell completely in love.
Gossip called them two lovey-doves.

This was too perfect, it couldn't last forever.
There soon came a girl that didn't make things better.
This girl was very jealous of the two,
So she formed a plan on what to do.

Out by the murky bog one day,
She took them and said they had a game to play.
Sneaking up behind them, she pushed the girl in.
He was devastated and yelled at the girl for her sin.

The sinner now had to live with the guilt
That she had ruined the relationship the two had built.
This sinner also now burns with shame
That she destroyed an everlasting flame.

Now, he waits, waits by that bog
Staring, staring through the fog.
He's waiting, waiting for the day
When his one true love will take him away.

Justine Lewis
Age: 12

Fall
World Series, football
playing, Thanksgiving, raking
In the fall I feel good about football.
Harvesttime

Jared Samuel Stone
Age: 10

COMPUTERS

C omputers are fun to play
O pen to use Internet
M ouse to click
P ut in CD-ROMs to play games
U se to find information
T o type stories
E nter your password
R un different programs
S urf the web

Katie Lee Collier

ALL AROUND THE WORLD

All around the world
All around I see
Everything on TV
Killing with no plea
I see you
I see me
I see friends and kids like me
Shooting each other like enemies
What will it take to make it stop?
A hug or a kiss or a pat on the back
To show you LOVE not HATE is in my heart

Danielle Gragg
Age: 12

MR. AND MRS.

Mr. and Mrs. sat on a pot,
catching candy through the slot,
reading the mail,
still sitting right there.

Mr. and Mrs. got up to go check on the pot,
to see if it was hot.
Mr. and Mrs. went to the lot,
to check if any food had rot.

Grant Nix
Age: 7

SUMMER

Flowers bloom
children play.
Little Boy Blue
runs away.
Some people hide
and some ride.
People pray
summer don't go away.
And that's the end
of everything
and most things
that rhyme.

Savannah Armour
Age: 10

JESUS

Jesus is up and down all around
anywhere and everywhere
but you know I see him like any other
of his creatures,
you see God in a whole different way
because you see God through your heart
and that's the way it will stay
forever and one day.

Kayla N. Turner
Age: 11

BEAUTIFUL MOUNTAIN

It's a mountain that takes your breath away,
Oh, I could sit here looking at it all day,
It's so big and beautiful and bright,
You would faint, when it got in your sight,
It has cliffs and snow and is very tall,
To me it's a new beginning, to others it's a wall,
As I sit here on this cliff,
A breeze blows in, and I catch a whiff,
Of that fresh spring air,
That lies on that amazing mountain.

Amber Gwin Seagraves
Age: 10

STARS

Stars are bright, shiny,
And different shapes.
Some constellations
Make them look like apes.

They are here at night
And run away in the day.
But I wish, I wish
They would stay.

Katie Joy Williams
Age: 9

FOREST FIRES

Forest fires
Sweet but smoky forest fire
Burning bright in the night.
Red, yellow, orange lights
Warm your face as you watch the sight.

The taste of burnt marshmallows comes to mind
When I taste the sooty air.
Snap, Crackle, Pop,
The wood explodes with sound.

William White
Age: 10

On Thanksgiving day we eat a feast.
   The food tastes very good to say the least.
After lunch we play ball.
   We play until we're about to fall.
We go back inside to sing
   Until our ears are about to ring.
To end the day
   Our family kneels to pray.

Keith Hardee
Age: 9

STONE COLD

'Round and 'round, in a haze
Every night waiting for you
You run hot, then you're cold
But this game you play
Is getting old.
Now it's time you learned,
With fire you're gonna
Get burned. And my heart
Is stone, I'd rather
Be alone.
Just turn and walk away.
There ain't nothing you can
Ever say. Nothing you
Do to make me stay.
After all, the love is gone, it's
Gone. I closed my eyes,
Pretend that there was nothing
Wrong. In my heart, in my soul,
I remember every lie you
Told. Now I stand my ground,
Never gonna turn around,
And my heart is stone,
I'd rather be alone.

Blake McDuffie
Age: 14

THE RED FLOWER

I
saw a
red flower in the yard
so I drew it
on a card.

Lauren Wright
Age: 8

THANKSGIVING DAY

Many years ago in a land far away.
Lived some people who weren't allowed to pray.
So they packed up all they owned
And rode on a boat at night.
To find a place to live and have equal rights.
They traveled and looked for a place to live.
They found a new land and thanks they did give.
They built homes and barns made out of logs and clay.
They worked many hours night and day.
The people looked around at all they had done.
They knew in their hearts they had finally won.
They said "Let's give thanks for the good of all man."
So now you all know how Thanksgiving day began.

Carrie Leanne Miller
Age: 12

CATS

C alm and clean
A mazing and active
T errific and tough
S killed and splendid

James Forrest
Age: 12

SUMMER

Summer is like the flowers
As bright as a city night
And like the spring
From time to time.

Brandon Michael Hanley
Age: 10

THE MILLENNIUM

In the year 2000
Maybe they will discover a new planet
Maybe there will be life on the planet.
They may even build a new space station
People will live on it like they do on earth.

Ben Agnew

SOCCER

Soccer season is now gone
But I sure had a blast.
There were no games postponed.
I wish it would always last.

Year before last we were the best.
We were undefeated
This year we could not rest
Against the teams we greeted.

We all had lots of fun
And that's all that mattered.
Most of the time we were running,
But all the girls just chattered.

Jace E. Dalton
Age: 11

SURROUNDINGS

The sun shone bright
On the warm afternoon
As fall was slowly creeping through the air
My spine tingled as a cool breeze was making its presence
For I knew that the trees would soon be bare.

Jennifer K. Reed
Age: 12

THE PERFECT CHRISTMAS

Once on a pleasant snowy Christmas Eve,
There was a tree that stood so tall,
Ready for the things Santa would leave.
In the chimney became a sound,
Then Santa popped out and left gifts on the ground.
Santa patted his tummy and left with a wink,
For it was almost dawn when the sky was pink.
And in the morning the children came down,
Their mouths left a smile as they glanced at the ground.
And outside which was full of snow,
Their ears listened to a soft HO! HO!

Matthew Boggs
Age: 11

PLAYSTATION

I'm playing my Playstation,
I feel like fighting on a space station.
My favorite games are Spyro, Crash Bandicoot,
and Driver.
My Playstation means a lot to me.
There is no end to what you can be,
on a Playstation.

Erik Seabolt
Age: 12

STARS

Very hot and bright.
Can be a constellation.
Are very pretty.

Jack Edward Garrison

WHEN I DREAM

When I dream, I dream thoughtfully.
About things like palm trees, on a beach,
when the sun is going down.
About discovering treasure
and strange little people from underground.
I dream of candies and chocolates
of red roses and bright stars,
of meeting weird green aliens
from Jupiter and Mars.
I dream of flying with the birds
and of all the animals speaking human words.
And soft, blue, puffy clouds
and big white birds squawking very loud.
And messages in bottles that floated to the beach,
from way afar, from other kids,
across the world, I'll never see.
All these things I see and do, when I dream.
Dreams might come true.

Autumn Lee Kinsey
Age: 11

PEACEFUL MORNING

A light breeze
  Ripples like waves
Across the luscious meadow

The rising sun
  Shines happily
Across the colorful mountain

Morning dew
  Makes the meadow gleam
Brighter than the golden sun

Birds singing
  Adds a musical touch
To the peaceful morning

Nicole Bradley
Age: 11

FALL

Fall
October, Halloween
scaring, raking
It makes me feel excited.
Pumpkins

F. David White
Age: 10

On the way to the park
I was riding my bike.
When faster than light
popped up my spotted dog Spike.
Faster, faster, faster I sped,
not knowing the danger coming ahead.
I did not dare to look
helpless as I could be.
Going fast as I could,
I crashed into a tree.
I picked up my bike
and called for my little dog.
We had to walk all the way home
in the dark fog.

Jessica Sargent
Age: 11

JUST ABOUT ME

My name is Harli.
Don't call me Charlie.
I'm from the U.S.A.
I was born on Memorial Day.
Speeding down the road on my Harley Davidson is fun,
But most of all, I like to run.
Please don't weep,
Because now I have to go to sleep.

Harli Bridges
Age: 10

OCEAN TREASURE

I went to the ocean
all happy and gay,
to sit and feel
the ocean's soft seaspray.
I waded into the water
it was icy and cold,
I reached down and discovered
a chest full of gold.
I swam back to shore
with my newfound treasure,
I opened it up
and much to my pleasure,
everything in it
was shiny and bright,
it all seemed to sparkle
with a lustery light.
It had bracelets and pearls
and necklaces galore,
it made me want to go back
to the ocean and explore.
From then on
I have found many things,
that bring me great joy
and all sorts of good tidings.
My poem is ending
as you can see,
I hope it was as fun for you
as it was for me.

Kathleen Renee Ragan
Age: 11

I like to read books,
On the couch I sat,
While my mom cooks,
I hear the eggs splat,
So I read some more about a fruit bat.

Brody Ferguson
Age: 11

Ants,
little bugs that like to invade
    Spiders,
little bugs with legs of eight
    Centipedes,
little bugs that crawl around
    Cockroaches,
little bugs I squish on the ground
    bugs,
little things with many legs
    bugs,
little things that live in logs
    bugs,
little things that eat raw eggs
    bugs,
All the bugs in the world
    bugs,
Are probably made to scare girls
    Bugs

Justin Moore
Age: 12

SCORPIONS

They creep at night in fright!
They crawl on eight feet.
They don't eat meat!
And they scare with all their might.

Spencer Kinsey
Age: 8

MARY

Over the hill and far away
Mary played half the day
Then she went home and drank some water,
Then she went outside and played with her daughter.

Chaz Sosebee
Age: 8

PUMPKIN

Pumpkin pumpkin round and fat
Will you grant me a wishes hat?
And a little black cat.
And a big gold rat.

Mark James Moody

Ninja
Strong, tough
They are great.
Makes me feel safe
Karate

Curtis Sheldon
Age: 8

SPORTS

Sometimes I play football.
I play football in the fall.
I have a soccer ball.
In soccer they like to maul.
Sometimes I play basketball,
So does my friend Paul.
I like to play baseball.
It is very fun,
But when you hit the ball,
You really have to run.
If you hit the ball to first,
You shouldn't even try.
For I will get you out,
Even if you can fly.
I'm starting a new basketball season.
I like it, that's the reason.
Basketball is very rough,
Therefore my coach is very tough.

Benson Cantrell III
Age: 12

A MOOSE AT MY HOUSE!

We have a moose in our house.
We like to do things together.

Matthew Ware
Age: 6

TRAINS

Trains are fast
Trains are slow
Here is something good to know
Trains don't run off the line
Unless you give them a dime.

Tyler Penland
Age: 8

THE DAY BY THE BAY

One day I went to the bay,
And I found some hay.
At the bay that same day I found a hound.
The hound was brown.

Crystal Marie Rogers

EARTH

Fish, Atlanta, turkeys, hogs,
Pigs, cows, stores, and logs.
Hawaii, eggs, eagles, trees
Without these the earth would not be.

Dylan Schlandt
Age: 6

FRIENDS

Friends are nice
And friends are good.
Friends play
Like friends should.

Jordan Casper
Age: 6

I WOULD LIKE TO HAVE A RABBIT!

I would like to have a rabbit.
I would name it LaNora.
It would eat lettuce and carrots!

Katie Penick

A PIRATE

A pirate has a patch.
A pirate steers the ship.
A pirate has a sword.
And that's the way a pirate's life goes!

Levi London
Age: 7

THE DEEP BLUE SEA

Dolphins swim, crabs crawl,
it's so much fun to watch them all.
The ships row on with their crews,
can't you see the ocean blue?
The tides roll in,
while turtles glide by,
It's all so great I want to cry.
People play on the beach,
as whales set out to breech.
As sand castles dot the shores,
the sea creatures finish up their daily chores.
As the sun begins to set,
while some creatures are going to bed,
others are just waking up their sleepyheads.
The day is through,
but as you knew,
tomorrow is another day in the ocean blue.

Dee Cantrell
Age: 16

THE PEACEFUL WALK

Along a path are flowers and trees,
Where the wind blows a peaceful breeze,
The sun seeps through the newly-grown leaves,
And the lake laps against the shore.

Two little boys and their father sail,
A grandmother sits on a bench so frail,
A squirrel scampers around and shakes its tail,
While a cat lies in the sun.

A butterfly glides through my view,
The sky is so vibrantly blue,
With only a fluffy cloud or two,
While a bird jumps from tree to tree.

A little girl and a puppy play,
Everyone is very gay,
What a joyful and wonderful day,
The first day of SPRING!

Christi Lee Nesmith
Age: 12

THE MEANING OF LIFE

The meaning of life,
Is to do your best,
To strive so hard,
You pass the test

To see the light,
From up above,
The holy light,
All filled with love

The meaning of life,
Is to let Heaven reign,
And not to worry,
About what you lose and gain

To beat the odds,
The hard times, the pain,
Just to feel safe
At home again

To make sacrifices,
Just to help another,
To know your life was worthwhile,
On our earth, our mother

That is the meaning of life.

Nicholas Bradley
Age: 11

THE DAY

On the day I went to the bay
I saw a stray.
It stayed at the bay
For a very long day.

Chanda Dockery
Age: 8

MY CAT

I have a cat
It sort of scares me.
I play with my cat
When he is in the kitchen.
He sometimes plays too rough
That's why he had to move away!

Brittany Riley

THANKSGIVING

T hank you for my stuff.
H appy holiday!
A pple pies
N ice food
K ind
S hare
G iving thanks to God
I vy
V ery good
I love it!
N o more school for three days!
G od

Connor Timpone
Age: 7

SUN GLOW!

Sun glow at morning.
Moon glow at night.
Sun glow is tall.
Sun glow is small.
Sun glow is bright.
Sun glow is light.
Sun glow is nice!

India McCoy
Age: 7

DAISY

My dog is lazy.
Her name is Daisy
She jumps on me.
She's filled with glee
On her chest it looks hazy.

Jake Panter
Age: 11

DISNEY WORLD

Down in Orlando, there's a place that's fun,
Where magic begins in the hot sun.
People come all year,
Goofy they come to hear.
People are sad when the day is all done.

Emily Bennett

A SPIN ON THINGS

When I look into the eyes of my generation
I see anger and rage
the love that we used to have is diminished as
we turn the page
"Equality among people" has turned to
"Fight for your own"
"I love you dear" has turned to
"Don't use that tone"
Racism and prejudging are
a mask for insecurity
Creativeness and the "unique you"
are crushed by maturity
Cynicism has entered the minds
of the young
Therefore all of our individualism
has been hung
Our wrists are scarred as
are our souls
My dilemma reminds me of those
burning coals
At first jumping with joyful
flame
The determination of the fire you
cannot tame
As this energetic coal ages
and reforms
All of the love and fire has been
burned
Burned to nothing but soot
and ash
And so your entire flame is gone
in a flash

Self-respect and opinions are
compromised
Sometimes justice helps you out
and cuts them down to size
In conclusion be who you
be
But then again don't listen
to me
Just when you're tired of being
a shell
When you've finally decided pretending
is Hell
That's when it's your choice to listen
to my advice
If you walk all over people you'll eventually
pay the price

Stephanie M. Thornton
Age: 15

BLUE

Blue is the color of a pool.
Blue is the color of a T-shirt.
Blue is a piece of paper.
Blue is a writing pen.
Blue is as colorful as the shiny sky.
Blue is a blueberry.
Blue is a color.

Ethan Stinchcomb
Age: 7

WEEPING WILLOW

Weeping willow
stop your crying
it is gone now.
The singing birds,
the laughing children,
the warm days of August,
our singing in the days,
in the sun.
Your leaves are gone,
your smile is gone,
and so are your
loving children.
Weeping willow,
stop your crying,
we will play again soon.
The children will laugh
and you will smile.
Weeping willow,
stop your crying...
the summer...
is gone.

Elizabeth Dunn
Age: 11

THE CAT AND THE MOUSE
AND THE MOUNTAIN!

The cat sat on the mouse.
The mouse sat on the cat.
The cat and the mouse sat on the mountain!

Taylor Leigh Skelton

Ted Williams
Talented, determined, hardworking
He led Boston to the American League
His mother's name is May, and brother Danny
He was on his high school baseball team
WWII he was stationed at Pensacola Naval Base
The Splendid Splinter

Emily Karst

Glenn
shy, handsome
playing, swimming, running
happy, silly
Blake

Glenn Blake
Age: 8

Y ogi
O rdered a new uniform and more pay
G reat baseball player
I nspired the Yankees

B aseball made him live an
E xciting life
R un fast
R un for home plate
A warded MVP three times

Dana Parker

THE ARMY

I plan to build an army
that no one else has built.

I'll make a million robot soldier creatures
and arm them with words.

They will be strong, sturdy.
They will form a rock.

We will worship God.

Samuel Jacob "Sam" Justus
Age: 7

DAD

My dad is a carpenter and works with his hands.
My dad's hands are scratched, beat-up and rough,
But his hands are still comforting and loving to me.
Even though he is tired and his back is aching,
He still finds time to play basketball with me.
When I am hurting, he is always there beside me
With his hands, they are comforting and loving to me.
My dad is one out of a million.
I love my dad and he loves me.

Jesse Andrew Carter
Age: 11

COLUMBINE

I woke up one morning as happy as could be
My mom fixed me breakfast and handed me the key
She said good-bye and went on her way
The way things were going it would be a wonderful day

I walked to the bus stop along with all my friends
I didn't know then, that this could be my end
When we arrived, we walked in the school
Making sure to act really, really cool
I found the library, where I was to meet my best friend
To me she was more than "just a friend," practically kin

All of a sudden, I heard someone scream
I turned and I saw an unfamiliar thing
He's got a gun I heard someone yell
I tried to run but my legs turned to gel

I shouldn't be here, my mind made me think,
It's all just a dream, then I heard some more screams
Oh my God, there it was, a real live shot
There was nothing I could do, I felt like a tot

Just then my best friend screamed
He's got that gun pointed at me!
I turned and watched as she begged for her life
All I could do was join her in the fight for her life
He said OK, and I was relieved, but, Oh my God!
Now it's pointed at me

I did not have a chance to say good-bye
He pulled the trigger as I asked myself why

The last thing I saw was my best friend cry
"Oh my gosh why must she die?"

I felt it hit and I saw blood spatter
But it was over before you could say mad hatter
As I lay there dead I saw her fall
An angel that was not so very tall

She whispered it's going to be all right
And I said good-bye as I rose out of sight

A. Elyse McGregor
Age: 13

MY ANGER!

Anger beats me!
It looks like fire.
It smells like toast burning to a crisp!
It sounds like thunder!
I'm big-time mad!

Edward Kalkreuter

MEMORIES

Day by day we tried to reach you.
Although no one else did,
Somehow I always thought you'd pull through.
You were so far away, but yet so close to me,
And it seems you've been gone for so long,
I've forgotten how our life used to be.
What a relief it was to hear the sound of your voice.
Now, we know this tragedy wasn't your choice.
"What's wrong with her, God?" as we often did ask.
"Why doesn't she speak? Why doesn't she laugh?"
"A disease of the brain," the doctors had said.
Not in your heart, but all in your head.
As you angered me with so much worry
That I couldn't see,
I finally discovered just how much you meant to me.
As I lay in my bed and continued to cry,
I hoped and prayed that you wouldn't die.
But, yes, this nightmare did come true,
And now I have nothing but dreams of you.
Some are happy, some are not,
But I still find you unhappy in them a lot.
Marilyn, there's one thing that I clearly see,
Now you are a memory.
A memory that I will cherish and dream of
For the rest of my nights,
And I will never forget being with you December 23rd,
When you lived the last night of your life.

Ashley Brooke Carpenter
Age: 14

HANGING OUT

H aving fun
A ll on our own
N o parents
G irls, look out!
I gnore the rules
N o turning back
G oing over the top

O ver the top
U nder the wire
T onight!

Chris Scott

HOG

The farmer once had a dog
And he named it Hog,
And once in the fog
He chased a frog.
Once he jumped over a log
On the day of sog,
Then he tried to bog
When he broke a cog.

Joey Conard
Age: 7

COLORS

Black is a cat that's my pet.
Black is a crayon I color with.
Black is a dog that's my pet.
Black is a square on a checkerboard.

Orange is a Popsicle I eat.
Orange is a carrot I eat.
Orange is a goldfish that swims.
Orange is a pencil I write with.
Orange is a crayon I color with.

Purple is a pencil I write with.
Purple is a crayon I color with.
Purple is a chair I sit in.
Purple is a cookie I eat.
Purple is a curtain that hangs on my window.

Green is a Christmas tree I use at Christmas.
Green is a sour juicy grape.
Green is a rubber snake I play with.

The sky up high is blue.
The speeding car is blue.
The shirt I wear is blue.
The book I read is blue.
The hat I wear is blue.

Brown is a file cabinet I look in.
Brown is a clock that ticks.
Brown is a desk my teacher sits in.
Brown is a speaker that is very loud.

Red is a robin I take a picture of.
Red is a watermelon I eat.
Red is a shiny apple I eat.
Red is a table I work at.

Yellow is a flower I smell.
Yellow is a convertible I drive.
Yellow is the sun that is very hot.
Yellow is a rubber duck that squeaks.

Pink is a heart on Valentine's Day.
Pink is icing that goes on a cake for my birthday.
Pink is an eraser I erase with.

Gold is a star I put on the Christmas tree.
Gold is a half a dollar I spend.
Gold is a statue that belongs to a rich kid.

Ashley Lewallen
Age: 7

BLUE

Blue is as beautiful as the sky.
Blue is the water, in the sea.
Blue is the taste of a wonderful blueberry that I eat.
Blue is most of our colorful earth.

Bennett Garner
Age: 7

Thanksgiving
happy, fun
eating, drinking, cooking
once every single year
Holiday

Justin Kane Kelly
Age: 9

NIGHT JOURNEY

As I watched through the night
There was a twinkle in it.

And the wind rustled
Against the soft grass.

I called my loyal cat
To take me on a ride through the sky
To see what else was there.

We saw Mars, we saw the sun,
We saw Saturn and Pluto, Mercury
And Jupiter, Venus too.

Then we came back to Earth
And landed on a bunch of cattails.

Sarah Ethel Kristin "Sally" Justus
Age: 6

$$IF I HAD A MILLION$$

I f I had a million, I would spend it all
  and not leave any at all.
F ly to the farthest place and cruise around the mall.

I 'd invite all my friends to a Friday night party.

H ave a hydro hopping competition at Harrison Square
A nd invite all the guys from the neighborhood.
D ance to some songs all night long.

A nnounce all the activities around the area.

M ake a competition and see who's the master of masters
  at the mat
I would announce the winner and give them a million too.
L ater in the day, have a Lamborghini race.
L ay out some BBQ on the grill. Have a great meal.
I t's time to end the party and tell everyone to leave
O pen your eyes and realize
N ow's the time to get up. It was just a dream.

Ricardo Martinez

S pent off-season with wife and nephews
H elped raise two nephews
O ften carved his own bats
E ntered pro baseball with Carolina Association in 1908
L oved to tell of the art of baseball
E ager to tell others of a man's honor
S cornful, was not his attitude
S our, he was not

J uly 16, 1887 was his birth
O ld he was, as he died at sixty-four
E mbarrassed when he received "Shoeless Joe" nickname

Brittany Dodd
Age: 12

FLOPPIES

A floppie's a thing that knows how to talk,
Knows how to eat, knows how to walk.
It has twenty-three pockets and violet hair,
Does it have violet eyes? I don't know. I don't care.

If you want to see one you'll have to look,
You will probably see it in a good book.
Maybe adventure, maybe mystery,
Or most likely you'll find it in a book with history.

Joni Avery
Age: 10

J ust an ordinary black man they said
A fter he signed with the Dodgers,
   they bowed their heads
C ame from U.C.L.A.
K ansas City was where he started
I n 1947 he was voted Rookie of the Year
E ven a movie was made about him

R achel Isum was his girlfriend
O n February 10 she became his wife
B orn in Cairo, Georgia
I nducted into the Army
N ew daughter named Sharon on January 13, 1950
S on named after him
O n October 24, 1972 he had a fatal heart attack
N o one could ever take his place

Phillip Martin
Age: 12

NATURE'S DANCE

Deep in the woods, quite a ways back
Deer played and ran through the brush
Their feet tapped the ground, touch after touch
It's a magical scene if you get a chance,
To see these beauties jump and dance

Martin Erbele
Age: 11

Dogs bark a lot.
If there were no dogs,
The bark wouldn't have been invented.
The dogs made the bark.

Russell Parnell
Age: 8

DESTINY

A life with you is a life with honor,
And to lose you is to lose my pride.
So many people, so little time,
But in my heart you're the destiny,
The keeper of the key to always win
And set me free.
To be so young and be so blind
Not to see how hard you tried
To love me -- tried to care,
But I would just act as if you weren't there.
I finally noticed, and you saw me
And made me feel like a beautiful flower.
I'm sorry I hurt you, let you down,
But I promise never to leave you
With no one by your side.

Amanda Anderson
Age: 14

CHILD

Still a child
Maybe so
But a child commands
Dreams of gold
Fields of lollipops,
Boundless love.

Still a child
That's not so bad
A child delights
In each warm sunray
The Chinese eye of a tabby cat
A paper kite floating high
Or Daddy's beat-up baseball cap.

Still a child
Thank God that I am
To see the mystery of life
Colored with a crayon blue
By the love of you.

Timothy Raymond Boyd
Age: 18

GRAVEYARD BY THE SEA

A perfect sphere of silver glow
Watching me as I watch below
A tunnel of clouds form around
Such a view from the ground
Reflecting rays
Jump off the waves,
And the mirror-like stones that mark the graves

Under the ground they sleep
Holding the secret that we all seek
The secret of what death holds
Those mysterious things which remain untold

The silence broken by rhythmic sounds
Of crashing waves and high rock around
The stillness of the air moved to-and-fro
From the salt-scented wind off the sea that blows

Near the edge of the cliff I stand
Clutching tiny grains of sand
No matter how hard you try
Through your fingers they find a way to pry
Squeezing tighter but they still get away
Falling towards the jumping spray

So much like dying
Clutching onto life while through your hands it's prying
Not wanting to let go
For fear of things we don't know

Through your fingers you watch it slip
Trying so hard to tighten your grip

Then you find that you can't win
You let life go into the wind
Down it falls to the waves
Into that sea of reflecting graves

Amanda Nelson
Age: 14

I LIKE CATS!

My cat is black and white.
He gave me a fright.
He likes cat food in his dish!
He does not like mice.
He does play in the grass.

Jordan Shepherd
Age: 6

TURKEYS

Turkeys are brown,
Turkeys are neat.
We go turkey hunting
For Thanksgiving and
Invite people over to eat!

Quinn Adamson
Age: 6

I THOUGHT

If I don't think a thought and didn't say a word.
If I didn't breathe on air or have a sound be heard.
If I never felt a warm summer breeze.
If I never caught a cold or heard someone sneeze.
If I didn't see a sight or smell a smell indeed.
If I didn't hear something go rumbling through the trees.
If I never live a life so lively as I please,
Just answer me one question,
Would I really be me?

Ashley Rainwater
Age: 8

G reat athlete
R eceived the Cy Young award four times
E xcellent pitcher
G rateful to his family

M any people admire him
A n all-around great player
D oes his best every game
D etermined to win
O f all players, he received twenty out of twenty-four
   first-place awards in 1992
X tremely dedicated

Lindsey Boddie
Age: 12

REPORT CARDS

Report cards, report cards are really a pain.
I just hope my report card lands in the rain.
If it doesn't then I won't get my way,
'Cause my mom will ground me a lot more
Than just one day!!!

Chase Dorsey
Age: 8

MY TEACHER

This is for my teacher:
Although sometimes you have to be tough,
We know you are as sweet as a preacher.
You should be proud of all you have done,
Hold on a minute, I've just begun.
You are sweet as can be from your head to your shoes,
We can't help it Mrs. Bennett,
We all love you.
You're teaching us well and making us smart.
I'll be sad the day we'll have to part.
Now as I bring this to a closer,
You should win teacher of the year a dozen times over.
So jump for joy,
Get off your keister,
I can't help it,
I love my teacher.

Jackie Marsingill
Age: 9

SAD

S hy
A ngry
D isappointed. This is how I feel when I am sad.

James Dustin Little
Age: 10

THANKFUL

I'm thankful, I'm thankful, I'm thankful to be alive
I'm thankful to have clothes on my back.
I'm thankful to have my brother, mother, and father.
I'm thankful to have a roof over my head.
This is what I'm thankful for.

Jessica Nicole Willis

TIME MACHINE

I wish I had a time machine,
to take me to-and-fro.
One that takes me back into the time of James Monroe,
or maybe the time of Paul Revere.
Oh, that would be a very fun year!
And what about the Alamo,
with Daniel Boone to see?

When I get home I'd show my mother
she'd be so proud of me!
And then I'd take my brother
for a trip in my time machine.

Leigh Elizabeth Nash
Age: 10

JEALOUS

Jealous to tell me why,
You are so mad at me.
Is it because of my clothes,
Or my new globe?
Is it because of my new shoes,
Or is it because I found my teacher's clue?
Please tell me why you're jealous of me,
Or, do I need to wait and see?

Kerchondra "Tori" Burden
Age: 11

SHADOW

Shadow,
My little black lamb,
I can still see you,
But you're just a dream,
I love you so much.

Shadow,
The day I got you,
You were so afraid,
You would hide in a corner,
Every time I came near.

Shadow,
Your distinct bleat,
Your beautiful brown eyes,
The way you stomped your foot,
I miss it, all.

Shadow,
I know you're gone,
For the rest of my life,
But it's okay,
We'll both get through it.

Shadow,
I can't wait,
'Til we're together again,
So we can run and play,
Just like we used to do.

I miss you
My little Shadow

We'll be together,
Just you wait and see,
Until then, I love you!

Tiffany Harvey
Age: 13

APPLE

Sweet, smelling apple
Crunch! Yummy hard, red ball
Juice dripping, gross core

Laurel Nason
Age: 10

JEALOUS

J ealous is more than mad.
E ven more than sad.
A t the time that you are jealous
L oving and caring is the way you
O bviously should be.
U p high in a tree house...
S trange things will happen, you won't
  be jealous you will be happy.

Kailyn "Claire" Rosser
Age: 11

School
fun, happy
working, learning, playing
jolly as a bee
Teacher!

Samantha Nicole Gaddis
Age: 9

WHY?

The dove soars across the baby-blue sky
So beautiful in my sight
Tell me why I can't fly that high
I really want to know.

God gave them wings,
And fearless flight.
I got only arms and legs,
And a fear of heights.

So one night I dreamed,
That I asked God why?
Why didn't you give humans the ability to fly.

He smiled and lovingly answered
You don't have wings,
Because you are always in the palm of my hand.

Jean Johnson

GREEN

The perfect appearance of freshly-cut grass
no tuft uneven.
The awakening sound of the bird's chirps
on a bright new day.
The fresh scent of lofty pine trees standing tall
in the dark forest.
The sweet taste of a newly grown apple crisp, juicy.
Green is the smooth feeling of the outer skin
of a tender pear smooth, perfectly even.

Victoria Loureiro
Age: 13

ZED

My name is Brett.
I have a pet.
His name is Zed.
Zed! That's what I said.
He has no teeth in which to chew.
But try telling that to my shoes.

Brett Funderburk

ALL AROUND

Green and yellow
Red and brown
They're all around
They're in the tree,
They're on the ground,
They're all around.

So pile those leaves
And swing them around,
They're so round
They're on the ground.
At night and at day,
We see them when we play
They're little things on the ground,
They're all around.

Christy Bates
Age: 11

RED

Red can be found in many places.
It can be found even upon some embarrassing faces.
You'll find it on fruit, clothing, and cars,
And even way up on Mars.
When you look at the leaves in the fall,
You'll see why red is my favorite color of all.

Jessica Moon
Age: 8

SHARKS!

Sharks --
I don't
know much about them.
I do know that they are man-eaters.

Ryan William Steiner
Age: 9

BEES! BEES!

BEES! BEES! They're in the trees,
BEES! BEES! They're in the leaves,
BEES! BEES! They're in the seas,
BEES! BEES! They are in my sight,
BEES! BEES! They are just so tight.

Justin Watts
Age: 10

MY PET

My
pet is funny.
He runs around the room
and goes outside
and plays.

Christie Miller
Age: 8

RAINBOWS

Rainbows
are pretty.
They are colorful.
You can find gold
if you look under them.

Jessie Margaret Evans

OLD JOE

Old Joe
Has a big toe.
He came from the South
He has a big mouth.
The hair on his head
Is a very bright red.
His old shirt
Has a lot of dirt.
He lives in a funny house
That has a gray mouse.
He has a fat hog
That lies on a huge log.
And that's the story of Old Joe.

Peyton Floyd
Age: 7

SCHOOL

School is not exactly cool,
In fact some people even fall asleep and drool.
We sometimes get to do puzzles,
But at least we don't have to wear a muzzle.
There are a lot of things to make it better,
But at least we don't have
To make a green and purple sweater.

Rebecca Middlebrooks
Age: 10

SCHOOL

School is a place where I go to learn
It is a place where you can't get burned
Sometimes I like to go
But sometimes I go really slow.

Sherry Ann Greenway
Age: 9

COTTON CANDY

My cotton candy is blue
It sticks to me
It will stick to you.
It starts to melt when I chew,
Even my tongue changes to blue.

Maxwell Moss
Age: 7

MOM

She is the one who is the cook.
She is the one who reads a book.
She is the one who is nice.
She is the one who drinks with ice.
She is the one who is filled with love.
She is the one who looks like a dove.
She is the one who loves me.
She is the one who makes gravy.
She is the one who stands tall.
She is the one who is above all.

Cody Buffington
Age: 11

HALLOWEEN

When Halloween is near,
People act weird,
Some people scare others down the street,
Some wear big clown feet,
Parents tell their kids,
"Let's go to the next house."
One girl looks like a mouse!
Some kids walk all night,
Some will get a fright!

Jessica Gray
Age: 9

ME!

E lliott
L ikes music
L earns well
I ntelligent
O utstanding student
T akes time
T alented

D ad's favorite
O utstanding goalie
Y oung
L oves pizza
E njoys sports

J ared's friend
O utgoing
H ates snakes
N ice
S on of Doy and Lynn
O utstanding friend
N ot dumb

Elliott Doyle Johnson
Age: 10

REVOLUTION

And the bombs bursting in air come back to life.
Men screaming showing that they want a free country,
independence, a big free world to explore
with some questions that we cannot answer
just like asking why a human being
would want to have a war.
Shots fired, men running, and stepping forth
to have the one country, the United States.
Cold, long, blistering winds blow
and freeze the soldiers' backs.
They push on trying and trying again.
Until a final battle, the very last one...

Katana Sherman White
Age: 10

FRIENDS

F un
R esponsible
I ntelligent
E nthusiastic
N ice
D o well in school
S mart friends

Chanel Cobb
Age: 10

C aring
R espectful
Y oung
S inger
T all
A ttitude
L oving

B ashful
R eader
O utstanding
W ell-behaved
N eat

Crystal Brown
Age: 10

CANDY

Candy is something you can find just about anywhere,
It can come in many forms,
It can be tart or sweet, soft or hard.
It comes in many different colors.
In a candy store, it's hard to choose
Red, yellow, green, orange, neon, purple,
And many, many more.
What would you choose?

Matthew Scott Ayers
Age: 9

SWEET SUMMER'S DAY

Running down the street,
Feeling the sun's heat.
Playing on a summer's day.

Kicking the ball and hitting the bases
Oh, what fun.
Ice cream and lemonade,
Couples on the porch.

Splashing in the pools
And sweet smell of barbecues,
Oh, the summertime!

David Joseph Evans
Age: 10

WHAT?

When I say something just out of the blue,
People say, "Why, who are you talking to?"

I give them an explanation that doesn't make sense.
Then they say,
"Are you in civilization or over the fence?!?"

Then I say, "What! Who are YOU talking to?"

Christy Seerley
Age: 11

WHAT A RIDE

We heard good things
  about the Morphis ride,
so we went down the escalator
    like a slide
      then we went outside,
        nobody was in line
so we gave the sign
    to hurry in line!
      It said to hold on
we were going down the track
  we stopped.
The track twisted
    turned
      twirled
        and whirled
    we turned the corner
    up
      up
        up
      uh
    uh
  uh
    upright again,
ran out of track
  and we were back!

Kyle Stewart
Age: 10

132

HUNTING CAMP

I like hunting camp at Thanksgivingtime.
The cold breeze blows and chills my nose.
I like to hunt deer but miss when they're near.
Oh, what a great season to hunt deer.

Devan Ashcraft
Age: 8

PETEY

Petey is my puppy
He is so cute
I only wish I could put him on mute
When he goes outside he runs around
Of course, I would never take him to the pound.

Jaclyn Reynolds
Age: 10

Malorie
Danceable, bold, kind, courageous
Sister of Jonathan
Lover of Rollerblading, dogs, fall festivals
Who feels excited about fall festivals, tired of my brother,
   hungry when I smell pizza
Who fears tornadoes, death, sickness
Who would like to see me when I get married,
   my Aunt Bea and Aunt Nale,
   my brother to be nice
Resident of Georgia
Burden

Malorie Burden
Age: 8

YOUR BODY

You have billions and trillions of nerve cells
They work just like you
They help you tie your shoe
While it rains in Spain
Cells make up the tissues of your brain
Excuse me, Madame,
Elements are substances made of one kind of atom
Let's go outside and run around
I'll teach you about compounds.

Sam Hilley
Age: 10

Will
Kind, naive, shy, hazel eyes
Son of Mark and Kim
Lover of TV, music, tigers
Who feels tired after doing homework,
    mad when my sister gets all she wants,
    hungry when I see chips
Who fears eating celery, snakes, tornado warnings
Who would like to see the Yankees
    win the World Series,
    Bulldogs win the championship,
    Cowboys win the Super Bowl
Resident of Georgia
Goldsmith

Will Goldsmith
Age: 9

THE MAN WITH THE VAN

Once a man
Had a neat van,
But it got stolen
Because it was rolling
Down the hills
With all of its thrills
And lots of meals.

Makala Morrison
Age: 10

Bobby
Green eyes, blonde hair, peach skin, kind
Youngest child in whole family
Lover of "Jurassic Park," cats, dogs
Who feels mad at his sisters, happy to go on vacation,
    happy to be on this planet
Who fears eating barbecue, eating celery,
    being lost in the jungle
Who would like to see my parents win the lottery,
    the Braves win the World Series,
    my mom to have twin boys
Resident of Georgia
Lewis

Bobby Wayne Lewis III
Age: 8

LIMES

Limes limes all the time,
Limes limes all the time,
Limes limes the clock chimes,
Limes limes all the time,
We eat them once on Monday,
And twice on Sunday,
We eat those limes all the time,
Limes limes with salt all over them,
Limes limes oh how I love them!

KeAndra Mattox
Age: 10

TIME

Time can be fast
Time can be slow
Time can even sit on a crow
Time can go under
Any little wonder
Of your little mind
But watch out
Time can make you blind
So now you see
How time can be

Mac McInerney
Age: 8

Cassie
Shy, special, knowledgeable
Youngest child of Angie and Carson
Lover of cats, "Bye, Bye, Love", and TAG
Who feels excited to go to the fall festival,
   tired of being grounded, curious about the millennium
Who fears snakes, watching scary movies, darkness
Who would like to see Backstreet Boys in concert,
   my grandma, my cousin
Resident of Georgia
Cleveland

Cassie Cleveland
Age: 8

MY DOG

My dog's name is Connan
We run and play when we can
We run in the fields
And up and down the hills
We have fun every day
Connan and I love to play.

Colt Bennett
Age: 8

ALL I CAN BE

I have to be
All I can be,
Not for you,
But for me.
To see all the
Oceans and seas,
I'm going to be
All I can be.
I don't have
To join the Army.
I don't have
To swim a sea,
I just have to be
All I can be.

Joanie Marie Pressley
Age: 13

THE BEE IN THE TREE

There once was a bee
Who lived in a tree.
He had to pay a fee
Because he couldn't live free.
His name was Eee
Golly gee, Eee couldn't see.
He had a friend named Zee.
Zee blew out his knee
When he flew into a tree.
Now Eee and Zee
Sit around and drink tea.

Abbie Strickland
Age: 8

BOOKS

I like to read all kinds of books,
Some about pirates with hands of hooks.
I like to read books about different sports,
Like tall players on basketball courts.
I like to read books of mystery,
But I don't really like ones about history.
I like to read with Mom each night,
Then she hugs and kisses me and tucks me in tight.

Logan Johnson
Age: 8

FOOTBALL

Football is fun
You get to run.
It's a great sport
You play on a field,
Not on a court.
You can play an instrument
It can be percussion or brass.
You don't play on cement
You play on grass.
Players get shirts
Cheerleaders get skirts.
That's how football works.

Stavantae Rucker
Age: 9

MY CAT

My cat's name is Dale
He likes to chase his tail.
He looks at me kind of funny
When I rub his tummy.
When I am feeling sad
He makes me laugh and feel glad.
I love my cat named Dale
Because he sure is swell.

Jeremy Lee Hughes
Age: 9

MOMMY, I SHRUNK MY BROTHER JAI

I shrunk my brother Jai
Because he bothers me every day,
He gets so much attention
I want him to go to detention.
My mommy will get so mad
She will tell my dad.
I will get in big trouble
Then I will have to pay double.
He is so small
I am really tall.
He looks kind of like a doll,
I wonder if he can play basketball.
Mommy, I didn't mean to
And that is all.

Jason Patel
Age: 9

SAMMIE

S weet and good at reading
A nd never ever starts speeding
M ost brilliant every day
M rs. Sammie's best friend is Fay
I think she's lovely, quite lovely
E specially her mother, who is quite special.

Samantha Kelley
Age: 9

JESSICA RAY

J umpy
E xtreme
S uper
S weet
I cy
C ute
A nd weird

R ough
A nalysis
Y ucky! Not me!

Jessica Ray
Age: 9

COLORS

I found a clue
On the glue
And it was blue.
My head
Was red
When I was in bed.
My pencil is yellow
Because I'm a good fellow.

Tyler Kesler
Age: 7

THE KEYBOARD

The keyboard sings with all its might,
Sometimes even through the night.
It seems to dance around the floor,
On the bed, and out the door.

The tunes it plays are oh, so dear.
It can even play when I'm not near.
Its hands are graceful, white and black.
It holds the music on its back.
Its legs are strong and firm indeed,
Its soulful music meets my needs.

Lauren Myers
Age: 11

A NOISE

A sweet sound going through my ear
Like a sweet woman calling me,
Or a sweet wind whistling for me,
Or the rain hitting the roof -- pitter-pat --
Or a summer day at the beach
With sea gulls and the waves hitting land
On the sandy shore,
Or it's my dream
Escaping through my ear;
So I go to sleep with it in my head.

Ian Little
Age: 8

JAKE

Jake is my dog
He eats like a hog.
He plays in the water
And he loves fish and frogs.

Leann Skelton
Age: 7

GRAPES

G rapes are great
R ipe grapes make excellent pies
A small fruit
P eople love to eat them
E asy to bite
S mall and good.

Ashley Fowler

MOON

Lighting up the sky.
Turning to face the sunlight.
Smiling all night long.

Zachary Lamar Hawks
Age: 9

THE YEAR 2000

The year 2000 has almost arrived
We will have no money, the bank will shut down
We will have no school
I think it is a lot of trouble
I think aliens are going to be here
That's what the year 2000 is about.

Natalie Brown

BIRDS

Flying in the sky.
Bringing food for their babies.
Teaching their children.

Sarah Robertson
Age: 8

N ovember is my birthday
O verall I like it the most
V ery little do I like the other months
E very day is fun in November
M ore and more impatient I get
B efore it will come
E specially on my birthday
R emind me when it is November 1.

Jennifer Lynn Robinson
Age: 11

October winds are getting cold
And you will see small animals
Retreating to their holes.
Frost is beginning to cover the ground
Pumpkins are getting big, orange and round.
School is in full swing but
Students can hardly wait until spring.

Justin Miller
Age: 10

HALLOWEEN IS COMING

Halloween is coming with ghosts and witches
Wearing costumes of bats and cats
And some with big black hats.
They will have lots of sweets
They will have their midnight treats.

Melody LeRoy

Holding my breath
counting to three
Why should I care
what they think of me
Glancing across
the dimly lit hall
To see my reflection
and how I appear
Placing my book bag
against the wall
Capturing the moment
that soon will be near
I do care what they think
Why should I change?
When I am happy being me.

Alia Noe
Age: 14

GREEN

I like green,
Because it's on my trees.
It's even in my eyes,
And sometimes it's on ties.
It's on a table where you play pool.
It's a good color to stay on at school.

Chantz Segraves
Age: 8

WHEN I TELL YOU I LOVE YOU
IT MEANS FOREVER!!

When I tell you I love you "it means forever"
I love you means that I accept you for the person
you are and do not wish to change you
into someone else.

"I love you means" that I love you when you're down
and not when you're just fun to be with.
I love you means that I love you
when you're too tired to talk.
I love you means I love you
when you have a bad attitude
not just when you're calm.

"I love you means" that I know your deepest secrets
and do not judge you for them
asking in return that you do not judge me for mine.
"I love you means" that I love enough not to let go
and to fight for what we have
and hope that you feel the same way too.
"I love you means forever."

Precious Ross
Age: 13

ON ALL HALLOWS EVE

One night on All Hallows Eve I saw such a sight.
That made me giggle with all my might.
And said wow what dancers? With glee in my eye.
And went off to find a way out.

Cory Chancey
Age: 10

People
unique, special
all so very important
caring, breathing, living
enjoying, everlasting, spiriting
nice, spectacular
Life

Bre'Auna K. Beasley

Rain comes as silent as day.
It smells just as good as fresh cut hay.
As good as a spring May morning.
As we sat in the classroom learning all day long.

Amber Bland
Age: 11

At last autumn is here
Umbrellas you might need
Together our families will stay
Under their warm quilts
While they talk about their school days

Allison Robertson
Age: 11

FRIENDS

F riends are good to have,
R elying on each other.
I 'm really glad I have friends,
E njoying time together.
N ew ones are fun to make.
D epending on each other when times are tough,
S haring things together.

Ashley Dobbs

TAYLOR CERTAIN

T alented student
A qua lover
Y o-yo lover
L aughter
O reo eater
R acer

C amera shy
E asygoing
R eal
T ourist
A pple eater
I gnored
N ice

Taylor Certain
Age: 9

FALL

When the leaves change colors
I know it is fall.
The wind starts blowing
The air gets cold.
I know summer has passed
And school is here at last.

Natalie Sanders
Age: 9

RAIN

Rain is pouring
no sun about
all the black clouds
letting out.
No kids playing
all indoors
waiting for
Mr. Sunshine
to come about.

Julianna Rae Cargle

SOFTBALL

This game is my life,
Sliding in the dirt,
Hoping you tag third,
Diving for ground balls,
Hoping you won't eat dirt,
Running around the bases,
Making smiling faces,
That is what the game is about.

Lauren Geisel
Age: 13

TROUBLE

T is for Trouble.
R is for Ryan.
O is for Other things I do.
U is for Understanding the difference
B is for Ball -- like football
L is for Lazy
E is for Every time I don't complete my work
  and I wish to start the day over.

Ryan Peloquin
Age: 9

CANAAN

C ool
A viators
N eed
A ir
A nd
N avigation

Canaan Richardson
Age: 9

BASEBALL

Baseball is fun.
Some games we won.
I like to catch all the pop flies at shortstop
Or a grounder when it takes a hop.
When you're batting, it is easy to strike out.
When you hit the ball your teammates shout!

Ryan Seerley
Age: 7

OH MY, OH MY, TODAY IS THE DAY

Oh my, oh my, oh my!
Today is the day!
I will be in the parade.
I will be sighted by my mom and my dad,
But I've got to take a bath
Or I'll smell bad.
But I do not have time.

Cody Phillips
Age: 8

THE CAT THAT CAN FLY

I once knew a cat
That could fly like a bat.
It flew away like a witch's hat
When it came down, it landed on a mat.
There it saw a mouse
And chased it through the house.
It hit its head on the bed
And then it was dead.

Zach Gambrell
Age: 10

LELAND TAYLOR

I am as smart as a scientist.
I am as loud as a boom box.
I am as crazy as a hyena.
I am as talkative as a telephone.
When I eat, I am as fast as a roadrunner.
When I draw, I am as good as Van Gogh.
I am as funny as a clown.
I am as good as an angel.

Dennis Leland Taylor
Age: 9

RAINDROPS

Rain droplets dropping down, dropping down,
Onto the ground.
No one knows where they may go,
No one knows where they may flow.
Oceans, lakes, or even streams,
They may go places we've never seen.
Dripping, dripping to the ground,
Rain is something that makes a beautiful sound.

Jessica Lee Higgins
Age: 9

MY BROTHER IS WEIRD

My brother is the weirdest person I know.
He walks upon his toe.
He has a fuss on the bus.
He's the weirdest person I know.
His name is Zach and he's really back,
From the pack of wolves, I know.
He climbs the wall and it's really tall.
He's the weirdest person I know.

Cadie Schofield
Age: 9

FRIENDS

F un
R un with friends
I love my friends
E nd of the year party and bring all of your friends
N o school
D elightful music at party
S o much fun!

Diana Maria Abreu
Age: 7

THE SEASON OF FALL

Thanksgiving is here.
Relatives are near.
Dad does the raking.
Mom does the baking.
Leaves are yellow, orange and red.
With Thanksgiving turkey we'll all be fed.
The parades are on, let's watch them all!
I really love the season of fall.

Matthew Robert Logano
Age: 9

SNAIL

Making a slime trail
Crawls slowly up the handrail
Hides under the nail

Heather Michelle Echols

SPACE

Shooting Stars   Flying Asteroids
What's out there?   Nothing

Fast Spaceships   Moving Planets
What's out there?   Nothing

Maybe Aliens   Maybe Super Novas
What's out there?   Nothing

    I'll tell you what's out there
        Everything!

Michael Grant
Age: 13

A LOVE UNIMAGINABLE TO ME

We will dance in our dreams;
We will hold hands on the beach;
We will know each other for who we are;
Our love will have no end.
We will love like a light that cannot die,
A love that is unimaginable to me.

I do not know him yet;
That's the hardest part of all,
Though I know it will all be worth it in the end.
I can almost hear his comforting voice,
Feel his arms about me;
I look forward to the day I meet
This love unimaginable to me.

Our hearts are already joined as one;
I will know the day we meet.
I will hear my heart and his heart;
They are on the same beat.
I want to see him, hold him, know him,
He, the love unimaginable to me.

I have seen him in my dreams,
Held him close,
Not been scared about the rest of my life,

knowing that he will never leave;
I have this knowing feeling deep in my heart,
   so please do not let me down.
I will have you in my dreams until I meet you,
The amazing love unimaginable to me.

Lauren Pfeifer
Age: 14

What a great soccer player I'd be,
I'll get past everyone,
What a great player I'd be,
Just watch me.

Tim Talford
Age: 11

When we eat on Thanksgiving day
I will have a good conversation with an Indian.
But first I will have to get ready.
Then I'll eat so much that I won't eat for another year.
I can't wait until Thanksgiving day is here.

William "Devin" Bailey
Age: 10

J im won the Cy Young award
I nteresting person
M ight be going to the Hall of Fame

A ngel's star pitcher
B orn September 19, 1967
B orn without a right hand
O verall he is a great player
T hinks about his family a lot
T errific baseball player

Charles Byrd
Age: 12

He thought her hair smelled as sweet
As the chocolate cake your mom makes.
The girl's hair was as blonde
As the hay in the field
That flies in the cold blizzard
Winter sky every day.

Stephanie Temples

On the playground
Lots of friends and our fun never ends.

We play on the monkey bars and the slide
When we play hide-and-seek
I always hide.

Katelyn Corbett

A FROSTY NIGHT

An icy wind blows
Across a frozen world
In the dead silence
Of the frosty night,
With the moonbeams dancing
Across the frozen, colorless ground.
The snow glistens and shimmers
Like silver glitter
Across the earth below.
Reaching for the heavens
For the dark sky above,
The bare trees tickle the stars.
From the branches
Clear icicles form
Reflecting and bending the light
Like a clear cylinder prism.
The moon is a bright night-light
That watches over us
As we sleep soundly.
Shadows play upon the snowy ground
Mimicking their owners like mirrors.
An owl gives a lonely hoot
Like a haunting moan
Which echoes throughout the land.
Frost forms on my window
Fogging the glass
Like God's freezing cold breath.
Looking out my window dreamily,

All that I see is the pale snow
Like a white wool blanket
Protecting the earth underneath.

Julie Shepherd
Age: 13

There sat the boy sitting next door,
Eating an apple core.
He was hugging a blue teddy bear,
sitting in his underwear.
I yelled put on some pants
before you get bit by some ants.

Natalie Louann Wommack
Age: 10

Easter
happy, exciting
visiting, getting, celebrating
Jesus has risen again!
Fun

Brody Dudley
Age: 8

OCEANS

Quiet, sleep, calm, windy
Shark swims, fish fast, always
Big, hurricane, run

Ashley Whirrell
Age: 9

MY MASK

Every morning when I awake,
I put on my mask of impersonation, acting, pretending.
It shields me from society,
My greatest nightmare,
My biggest fear.
I know I'm covering up the real me,
But I'm so terrified if I take it off
And reveal the true me,
The world won't accept me for who I am.
Deep in my heart,
I want to show you me,
But then I'll be so secluded, alone, and terrified.
Deep breath. Here I go.
Now my mask, my protection, my concealment, is gone
And you see me.
I'll try to be chivalrous, bold, hardy
And work my best at showing who I really am,
But in case the world turns away from me,
I'll keep my mask at hand.

Darcy O'Connor
Age: 13

MY OWN MAN

I'm my own man,
I do anything I can.
I do everything I please,
And I do it with the greatest of ease.

I can stay up 'til midnight or three or four,
And watch rated R movies with lots of gore.
I could eat candy by the ton,
That way it's simply more fun.

I can play video games all day,
Then go out and play.
As for chores,
I don't need such bores.

I could live on pizza and ice cream,
And eat forever, or so it may seem.
I can play ball in the house,
And forget to be "as quiet as a mouse."

I'm my own man,
I do anything I can.
I do everything I please,
And I do it with the greatest of ease.

I don't ever have to go to school,
'Cause I'm not a fool.
I could never set foot there,
Not even on a dare.

I can leave my toys in the living room,
Or leave my clothes on the floor of the bedroom.

No one to tell me what to do,
I can do all sorts of new stuff too.

I can throw a wild party late at night,
With balloons and streamers, I just might.
With punch and pretzels and cake and more,
Games, puzzles, riddles, and fun galore.

I'm my own man,
I do anything I can.
I do everything I please,
And I do it with the greatest of ease.

I can have mountains of toys,
Ones that blink, shake, and make noise.
I can watch Saturday morning cartoons
All weekend long,
Even ones with a cheesy theme song.

I could sleep in 'til noon,
I wouldn't be waking up anytime soon.
I could scribble with crayons on the wall,
Of the kitchen, parlor, and the upstairs hall.

Every day could be my birthday,
I would have presents galore, I just may.
I can sing and dance in the rain,
Without people saying "You're insane."

I can do anything I please,
And I do it with the greatest of ease.
'Cause I'm my own man,
But first I have to ask my mom if I can.

Brian Ingram
Age: 12

KITTENS

Playing with the yarn.
Chasing brothers and sisters.
Running from the dog.

Tosha Leah Simmons
Age: 8

WINTER

Winter is coming
This is the time for Christmas
Maybe it will snow

Emma Freese
Age: 9

HAPPY KITTENS

Happy kittens play
wildly and loudly
outside.

Chelsea Jenkins
Age: 7

MY FRIEND

M eek,
E ager to learn,
L oving,
I will always remember her.
S weet,
S haring with others,
A friend to last a lifetime.

Whitney Hope Furr
Age: 10

I love to watch the moon
It will come out soon
I've waited all day
And this is where I lay
Here in the afternoon

Paige Dooley
Age: 10

FRIENDS

Some friends are good ones
but you never know.
They can seem to be good
but they're not.
But you see, mine are.
I don't know, maybe they're great,
maybe they're bad.
I don't care,
because they are my true friends.

Jacqueline Marie Anderson
Age: 11